The Making of a Champion

A World-Class Boxer

Heinemann LIBRARY

Don Wood

www.heinemann.co.uk/library
Visit our website to find out more information about **Heinemann Library** books.

To order:
☎ Phone 44 (0) 1865 888066
📄 Send a fax to 44 (0) 1865 314091
💻 Visit the Heinemann Bookshop at www.heinemann.co.uk/library to browse our catalogue and order online.

First published in Great Britain by Heinemann Library, Halley Court, Jordan Hill, Oxford OX2 8EJ, part of Harcourt Education.
Heinemann is a registered trademark of Harcourt Education Ltd.

© Harcourt Education Ltd 2004
First published in paperback in 2005
The moral right of the proprietor has been asserted.

Editorial: Geoff Barker, Rebecca Hunter and Dan Nunn
Design: Keith Williams
Illustrations: Peter Bull
Picture Research: Rachel Tisdale
Consultant: Jim Foulerton
Production: Duncan Gilbert

Originated by Ambassador Litho Ltd
Printed in China by WKT Company Limited

ISBN 0 431 18937 4 (hardback)
08 07 06 05 04
10 9 8 7 6 5 4 3 2 1

ISBN 0 431 18947 1 (paperback)
09 08 07 06 05
10 9 8 7 6 5 4 3 2 1

British Library Cataloguing in Publication Data
Wood, Don
A world-class boxer. - (The making of a champion)
1. Boxing - Juvenile literature
2. Boxing - Training - Juvenile literature
I. Title
796. 8'3

A full catalogue record for this book is available from the British Library.

Acknowledgements
The publishers would like to thank the following for permission to reproduce photographs:

Corbis pp. **6, 7** (Bettman), **8, 9, 12 & 13** (Bettman), **14** (Colin McPherson), **17 bottom** (Dimitri Iundt), **20** (Randy M Ury), **23 top** (Michael Brennan), **33 bottom** (Pete Saloutos), **35** (Thierry Orban), **39 top** (Michael Brennan); Empics pp. **16, 24, 26, 30, 31, 37 top, 42**; Getty Images pp. **4** (Holly Stein), **5** (Jeff Haynes), **10** (Ian Walton), **11 top** (Stuart Franklin), **11 bottom** (John Gichigi), **15 top & bottom** (John Gichigi), **17 top, 19** (Holly Stein), **21** (Al Bello), **22** (Stuart Franklin), **23 bottom** (John Gichigi), **25** (Jed Jacobsohn), **27** (John Gichigi), **28 & 29 top** (Al Bello), **32** (John Gichigi), **33 top** (Paul Gilham), **34** (Al Bello), **37 bottom** (Al Bello), **38** (John Gichigi), **39 bottom** (Al Bello), **40** (John Gichigi), **41** (Al Bello), **43** (Kevin Winter).

Cover photograph reproduced with permission of Action Images/Alex Morton.

Every effort has been made to contact copyright holders of any material reproduced in this book. Any omissions will be rectified in subsequent printings if notice is given to the publishers.

Contents

A battle between giants   **4**

The origins of boxing   **6**

The Queensbury Rules   **8**

History of the
    world championships   **10**

Weights and measures   **12**

So you want to be a boxer?   **14**

The amateur world   **16**

Equipment   **18**

Training   **20**

The support team   **22**

Attack!   **24**

Defence   **26**

Developing a knockout punch   **28**

Sparring   **30**

Safety   **32**

Devising a fight plan   **34**

Scoring points   **36**

The day of the fight   **38**

The pain barrier   **40**

Being a champion   **42**

Boxing greats   **44**

Glossary   **46**

Resources   **47**

Index   **48**

Words printed in bold letters, **like these**, are explained in the Glossary.

A battle between giants

It is Sunday 9 June 2002, Memphis, USA, and the most expensive sporting event of all time is about to begin. The two boxing legends that stand face to face in the centre of the ring will earn a total of US$40 million. Reigning heavyweight champion Lennox Lewis of the UK is hot favourite to win, but his hard-punching American challenger Mike Tyson is determined to recapture the glory of his time as world champion. This is championship boxing at its finest, with two champions ready to slug it out to decide who is the toughest man on the planet.

Jabbing to victory

The fight begins slowly: punch after punch misses the target as the two fighters warm to the task ahead. Then, in the second round, Lewis unleashes the weapon that will ultimately decide the outcome of the contest. Lewis launches a series of punches that repeatedly connect with Tyson's unprotected head. As the rounds go by, Tyson begins to wilt. The man who terrorized the heavyweight division in the late 1980s is about to fall.

Down and out

In his heyday 'Iron' Mike Tyson was invincible. Opponents were lucky to last a round before being overcome by Tyson's relentless assaults. But all of that seems a long time ago. Spells in prison and long periods of inactivity have dulled Tyson's reactions. His face is a mask of blood. In the eighth round, a right-hand punch from Lewis knocks his opponent to the ground. The fight is over. Lennox Lewis is hailed one of the greatest fighters of all time.

A former undisputed heavyweight champion of the world, Mike Tyson was once the most feared boxer on the planet.

The world of boxing

This is what boxing is about: great champions competing at the highest level for the richest prize in their sport. But behind the glory of occasions such as this lie years and years of hard work and dedication. This book takes a look behind the glamour of boxing to give an in-depth view of what it takes to become a championship boxer. We will look at the history of the sport and examine the training routines of the great champions. If you've ever wondered just what it is like to lace up the gloves, you should get ready to discover the truth about one of the toughest sports of all.

During his June 2002 fight with Lewis, Tyson (right) could find no answer to his opponent's thudding left *jab* – by the third round he was already cut over his right eye.

The origins of boxing

Boxing is a very old sport. A crude form of fighting with fists was known to be popular in Ethiopia nearly 6000 years ago. From there the sport spread to Greece and throughout the Mediterranean. In 688 BC, boxing was added to the sports contested at the ancient Olympic Games and a basic set of rules was established. Instead of gloves, boxers wore leather thongs to protect their fists. As well as inventing the boxing ring, the ancient Romans refined the rules of boxing further. In doing so they also added a sharp bronze spur known as the *myrmex* or 'limb piercer' to the leather thongs, turning them into weapons.

The rebirth of boxing

The Roman form of boxing was brutal. Combatants would often fight to the death in contests staged in huge stadiums called coliseums. By 30 BC however, the *myrmex* had been banned in Rome and with the spread of Christianity, boxing almost disappeared in Europe. Boxing resurfaced in England in the late 17th century when the Royal Theatre in London became a regular venue for boxing contests. At this time, the sport was a mixture of wrestling and boxing – as well as throwing punches, boxers were also allowed to hurl opponents to the floor and jump on them!

This picture shows the leather thongs that Roman gladiators wore when boxing.

Date facts

In 1734 James Broughton devised the first rules of boxing and introduced boxing gloves, although these were only used in sparring practice sessions.

In 1838 The London Prize Ring Rules were introduced. Boxers now fought in a 24-feet-square ring enclosed by ropes. A knockdown ended the round, with fighters being given a 30-second rest and an additional eight seconds to move to the centre of the ring.

The first boxing champion

Things began to change when Englishman James Figg opened up a boxing school in London in 1719. There he taught the rudiments of self-defence and brought boxing into the public eye by challenging all-comers to beat him. As the first heavyweight champion of Great Britain, Figg never lost. One of Figg's best students was Jack Broughton. From 1729 Broughton reigned as British champion for 21 years and drew up the first formal rules of boxing. For this reason he is known as the 'father of modern boxing'.

Bare-knuckle boxing

The bare-knuckle era of boxing began in the mid-18th century and lasted until the late 19th century. As the name suggests, boxers fought without gloves and, instead of a ring, spectators would stand in a circle holding a piece of rope that formed the boundaries of the contest. Bare-knuckle boxing was a very popular sport both in Britain and the USA. Contests would sometimes last for hours and have hundreds of rounds. The greatest bare-knuckle fighter of all was America's John L. Sullivan (1858–1918). In a long career, the tough Sullivan fought hundreds of contests and was the last world bare-knuckle heavyweight champion before gloves were introduced into boxing. In his early years, John L. Sullivan was known as a meticulous trainer. By 1889, however, his weight had ballooned to 109 kg. In order to get in shape, Sullivan began a training regime with champion wrestler William Muldoon (see below) and lost 16 kg.

MR MULDOON'S HOME

RUBBING DOWN AFTER THE BATH.

SULLIVAN'S TRAINING QUARTERS.

RUNNING TO REDUCE WEIGHT

WEIGHING

PRACTISING FOOTBALL

A SHOWER-BATH

A SWEATER.

"FEEL MY ARM."

The training programme of John L. Sulllivan.

The Queensbury Rules

The introduction of the **Queensbury Rules** brought greater safety and respectability to boxing. They were first published in 1867 under the sponsorship of John Sholto Douglas, the ninth marquis of Queensbury. The new rules introduced boxing gloves, three-minute rounds, a one-minute break between rounds and a ten-second rest given to any boxer who had been knocked **down** by a punch. The Queensbury Rules were quickly adopted all over the world. The first heavyweight championship that used them was staged in 1892 between James J. Corbett and John L. Sullivan.

Modern rules

The Queensbury Rules are still in use today, although over the years new rules have been added. These include a twelve-round limit to fights; the **three-knockdown rule**, which automatically ends the contest if a fighter has been knocked down three times; and the **standing eight second count**, in which the **referee** temporarily halts the contest and gives a felled or injured fighter eight seconds to recover.

Also introduced was a ruling that allows judges to decide a contest on points scored during the first three rounds of a fight if a boxer is unable to continue as the result of an accidental **foul** from his opponent.

James J. Corbett was born in 1866 in San Francisco. Unlike other heavyweight boxers, Corbett was tall, slim and elegant. In 1892, Corbett was the winner of the world heavyweight championship in New Orleans, USA.

Richard Steele

Now retired, boxing's most famous referee was the USA's Richard Steele (seen above with Francois Botha). During his long career, Steele refereed more than 140 world title fights. Steele began his career refereeing in small halls in 1972. Although he was nervous, he knew that he had the ability to reach the top. 'There was no doubt in my mind that I could do the job,' says Steele. 'I was just scared. I was scared because I wanted to do a good job. But as soon as the bell rang and I got into the fight I was okay.'

Within four years Steele was refereeing his first world title fight. One of Steele's most controversial decisions came in 1990 when he stopped the fight between Mexico's Julio Cesar Chavez and the USA's Meldrick Taylor. Taylor was well ahead on all scorecards when Chavez knocked him down with only fifteen seconds remaining in the fight. Many thought that Taylor should have been allowed to continue.

Longest match fact

The longest boxing match in history was 110 rounds long. In 1893 Andy Bowen of New Orleans and Jack Burke from Pittsburgh fought for 7 hours and 19 minutes in New Orleans before the fight was judged a draw. Both fighters were too exhausted to continue.

History of the world championships

For many years there was no official world body to govern boxing. World champions were usually 'linear', meaning that the current champion had beaten the previous champion. Then, in 1920, the National Boxing Association (NBA) and the New York State Athletic Commission began to sanction fights on the basis of rankings. The NBA changed its name to the World Boxing Association (WBA) in 1962 and began to dominate world boxing.

Governing bodies fact

Dates when boxing's main governing bodies were formed:

1920 National Boxing Association (NBA)

1962 World Boxing Association (WBA)

1963 World Boxing Council (WBC)

1982 International Boxing Federation (IBF)

1988 World Boxing Organization (WBO)

1992 International Boxing Organization (IBO)

The alphabet men

Nowadays there are sixteen recognized weight divisions in boxing and at least a dozen governing bodies. These include the IBF, WBO, WBF, IBC, IBA and WBU. Known as the 'alphabet men', all of these bodies have their own world champions in each weight division. This means that there are literally hundreds of fighters claiming to be world champions. One of the reasons for this chaos is the influence of television, which puts a lot of money into the sport and prefers to screen only world-title fights. Thankfully, public demand has encouraged boxing promoters to stage 'unification fights', with titleholders from different organizations competing to become the champions of more than one governing body at a time.

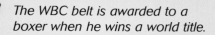

The WBC belt is awarded to a boxer when he wins a world title.

Don King

Boxing **promoters** are the people responsible for staging boxing matches. Their job is to match up fighters, hire the boxing venue, publicize the fight in the media and pay the boxers' purses or prize money. If a promoter is good at his job he can become very wealthy indeed – as in the case of America's Don King. The self-styled 'greatest promoter in history' has staged thousands of fights since he first worked with Muhammad Ali in 1972. He has worked with names such as Mike Tyson, Lennox Lewis and Evander Holyfield and is a millionaire many times over. Now in his seventies, the promoter shows no sign of slowing down, declaring: 'I'm going to retire when I go in my grave!'

The female touch

The 1990s saw the rise in popularity of women's professional boxing. Initially seen as little more than a joke, women's boxing quickly gained credibility. Fighters such as Britain's Jane Couch and America's Christy Martin proved that women are just as capable inside the ring as men. In a very short time female boxing governing bodies were established. These include the Women's International Boxing Federation (WIBF) and the International Female Boxers Association (WIBA). In women's boxing there are also sixteen weight divisions, but fights have a maximum of 10 rounds of two minutes' duration.

No Couch potato . . . Britain's Jane Couch has proved herself a fearsome competitor on the women's circuit.

Weights and measures

In the early days of boxing there were no weight divisions. This, of course, was very unfair to smaller boxers, who had no option but to fight much bigger men. It led to the establishment in the early 20th century of eight separate weight divisions, ranging in size from flyweight to heavyweight. This meant that lack of stature no longer prevented talented boxers from triumphing on the world stage. Over time, the number of weight divisions has been increased to sixteen in total.

Making the weight

Prior to entering the ring, boxers must be weighed in order to check that they have not exceeded their weight limit. Known as the weigh-in, this often takes place on the morning of the fight. As they climb on the scales, boxers wear as little clothing as possible. If a boxer fails to 'make the weight' he is allowed to return within two hours, by which time a brisk workout in the gym should have reduced his weight. If a boxer is still overweight after this period the fight may be cancelled.

Multiple champions

Although most boxers compete in only one weight division, there have been a number of fighters who have claimed titles in several different divisions. Because a boxer is competing against men who are naturally stronger than he is, winning titles in different weight divisions is a remarkable achievement. Recent multiple world champions are the USA's Thomas Hearns, Roy Jones Jr, 'Sugar' Ray Leonard and Evander Holyfield; and Mexico's Julio Cesar Chavez and Oscar de la Hoya.

At the weigh-in for his heavyweight title challenge against Sonny Liston (on the scales) in 1964, boxer Cassius Clay's outlandish behaviour shocked onlookers. Appearing to lose total control of himself, Clay (also known as Muhammad Ali) had to be restrained. Doctors were concerned that the boxer was 'frightened to death' by his huge opponent.

The Hurricane

Foremost among boxing's multiple world champions is America's Henry Armstrong (shown here on the right). Born in 1912, 'Hurricane Hank' was famed for his amazing stamina. He won his first world title at featherweight in 1937 and a year later moved up two divisions to claim the welterweight title. Later that year he moved down a division and won the world lightweight title. Incredibly, Armstrong held the featherweight, lightweight and welterweight titles simultaneously, an achievement that is unlikely to be repeated again.

The main weight divisions in boxing		
Division	**Weight range (up to)**	**Year introduced**
Light flyweight	108 lb / 49 kg	1975
Flyweight	112 lb / 50.8 kg	1913
Super-flyweight	115 lb / 52.2 kg	1980
Bantamweight	118 lb / 53.5 kg	1892
Super-bantamweight	122 lb / 55.3 kg	1922
Featherweight	126 lb / 57.2 kg	1890
Super-featherweight	130 lb / 59 kg	1921
Lightweight	135 lb / 61.2 kg	1896
Light welterweight	140 lb / 63.5 kg	1926
Welterweight	147 lb / 66.7 kg	1892
Light-middleweight	154 lb / 70 kg	1962
Middleweight	165 lb / 72.5 kg	1891
Super-middleweight	168 lb / 76 kg	1984
Light-heavyweight	175 lb / 79.5 kg	1903
Cruiserweight	195 lb / 88.5 kg	1979
Heavyweight	unlimited	1892

So you want to be a boxer?

Other sports are no doubt safer, but to many people there is nothing quite as exciting as boxing. This is what draws thousands of young men and women to the ring each year. But although boxing can be glamorous, behind every successful fighter are years and years of hard work and sacrifice. Any young hopeful who wishes to box must be aware that there is no short cut to fame and fortune. The art of self-defence is a skill that must be studied carefully for there to be any chance of success.

Fitness fact

In boxing, the most important areas of fitness to work on are:

- Endurance – This is achieved by regular runs, as well as body exercises supervised by the boxing coach.

- Strength – This is built up with sessions on the punch bag.

- Speed – This is improved during regular workouts with a speedball (a ball used for practising quick punches).

- Agility – Boxers improve their agility during regular sessions with the skipping rope.

Join the club

The first thing to do when deciding to box is to join a local **amateur** boxing club. Most boxing clubs operate at least three times a week. From the outset the boxer must be prepared to follow closely the instructions of the club's boxing coach. This means getting up early each morning to run, and undergoing an exercise routine that is designed to make the boxer extremely fit. In boxing, the aim is to hit and not be hit – to be able to do this successfully requires a very high level of fitness.

Despite having a disability in his hand, amateur boxer Gary Jarvie (left) enjoys a training session in his local gym.

Warming to the task

Before beginning an exercise programme it is important that a boxer's body is fully warmed up. A warm-up gives the muscles an adequate supply of blood so that muscles can contract properly. For this reason it is best to spend fifteen minutes running on the spot and shadow boxing. After the gym session is over it is also essential to 'warm-down'; light jogging and stretching will rid the muscles of stiffness.

Roadwork is the cornerstone of boxing – professional boxers run up to 5 miles a day, which can be especially taxing for the larger, heavier-muscled heavyweights.

The amateur world

Nearly every professional boxer has at one time boxed as an **amateur**. Some, such as Lennox Lewis, boxed hundreds of rounds as an amateur. For many years, amateur boxing was viewed as an 'ungentlemanly' sport, and it did not appear in the modern Olympic Games until 1904. Nowadays there are many national and international tournaments, including the Commonwealth, European and World Championships, which are staged every two years. The annual national amateur championships are known in England as the ABAs; in the USA as the Golden Gloves; and in Australia as the Australian Championships.

Amateur rules

Professional and amateur boxing differ considerably. In amateur boxing, contestants are required to wear a head guard at all times, as well as a protective vest. Greater emphasis is given to safety, with boxers given an **eight-count** after receiving a heavy blow – even if they remain standing. In amateur boxing there are four two-minute rounds and heavier 10 oz gloves are worn. This means that it takes more effort to throw punches, thereby reducing the risk of head injury. If a boxer receives three eight-counts the fight is automatically over. In contrast to professional boxing, knockouts are adjudged accidental and not the main objective of the fight.

Triple gold

Born in 1952, Cuba's Teofilo Stevenson (facing the camera) was one of the most famous amateur boxers. Stevenson represented Cuba in the 1972 Olympics and won a gold medal at heavyweight. He successfully defended his title at the 1976 and 1980 Games. Stevenson never turned professional and in 1976 he rejected an offer of US$5 million to fight World Heavyweight Champion Muhammad Ali.

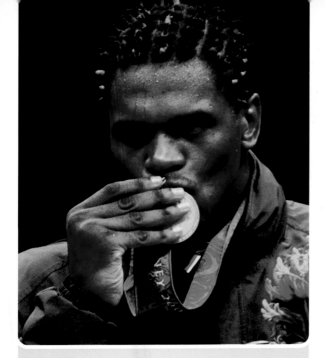
Britain's Audley Harrison, gold medallist in the 2000 Olympic Games.

Cuba fact

In Cuba professional boxing is illegal. There is, however, a thriving amateur scene that is organized by the state. This has enabled Cuba to become the USA's main rival in amateur boxing. In the Sydney Olympics in 2000, Cuban boxers won four gold medals.

Scoring points

In amateur boxing the winner of each round receives a maximum of twenty points. Extra points are also awarded for scoring punches – punches that connect with the chest or head of the opponent. During the fight, the judges each have two buttons before them – one for each boxer – and they press the appropriate button when they believe a boxer delivers a scoring punch. If a boxer commits an offence such as hitting below the belt or behind the head he loses points and receives a **warning**. After three warnings a boxer is automatically disqualified.

In amateur boxing, fighters are required to wear protective head guards and vests. The emphasis is on scoring points rather than knocking an opponent out. Scoring punches connect with the head or chest of an opponent.

Equipment

In the gym there is a range of equipment available to assist the boxers' training routine. Punch bags are made from leather and suspended from the ceiling; these help the boxers build up their power and learn to throw punches in **combinations**. Punch pads are large leather pads worn on the palm of the trainer's hands that help the boxers to get used to aiming punches at a moving target.

Boxers have to go to the gym five to seven days a week. Here there is a variety of equipment to improve their skills and conditioning.

Skipping fact

One of the most important items of equipment is also the cheapest – the skipping rope is used to develop speed and endurance. Some boxers become so good with the skipping rope that spectators come to the gym simply to watch them skip! Mike Tyson and Roy Jones Jr were modern boxers who both excelled at this skill.

Mouth protection

A **gum shield** is used by boxers to protect their teeth and gums. Without a gum shield the boxer would probably spend most of the time sitting in the dentist's chair! Gum shields are made of tough plastic. For an amateur boxer just starting out, gum shields can be bought in specialist sports shops. As the boxer grows in size the gum shield should be regularly changed. Many professional boxers have special gum shields made to fit exactly the contours of their mouths. Also essential is a head guard – most amateur boxing clubs keep a supply of these for boxers to wear.

Other equipment

Although boxing gloves are important, there are a number of other items of equipment that are also essential for fighters. These include:

- shorts with a correctly-fitting waistband, to avoid interfering with the boxer's breathing

- vests, which are usually worn by **amateurs**

- cotton socks, which help prevent blistering of the ball of the foot

- boxing boots with non-slip soles

- cotton bandages, which are wrapped around the hands for protection

- a ring robe, which keeps the body warm prior to a fight

- a **cup**, which is made of plastic and worn beneath the shorts in case of low blows.

Wrapping the hands

Hands are very delicate and easy to damage. For this reason boxers wrap their hands in bandages, which they wear beneath their boxing gloves. The fine bones at the back of the hand – or metacarpals – are particularly fragile, as is the thumb. Boxers are allowed to use a maximum of 5.48 metres of bandage, which is then held in place by adhesive tape.

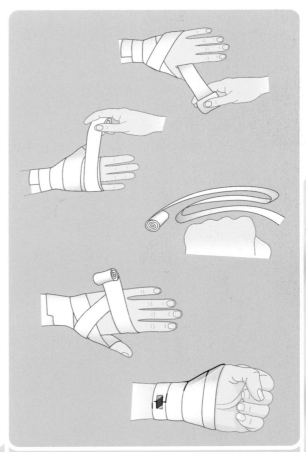

*There are different ways to bandage a boxer's hands, but all boxers are careful to protect the thumb and the back of the hand (see above). Before a fight, a boxer sends one of his **seconds** to watch his opponent's hands being wrapped. This is so no object can be hidden under the bandages.*

Training

In recent years great strides have been made in boxing training techniques. Nowadays boxing trainers are able to take advantage of modern research into physical conditioning. Boxing is an explosive sport: the act of throwing punches round after round while also defending against an opponent's punches makes boxing one of the most physically demanding sports of all. Boxers must be able to punch, slip and block with split-second timing – and continue to do so from the first round until the last.

Interval training

Boxing is an anaerobic sport: this means that the boxer, who is always on the move and forced to snatch breaths as and when he can, must exert himself with very little oxygen. This places the muscles under extreme duress. One of the most popular types of training used to counter this is called interval training. Intervals consist of intense sustained periods of exercise for a set period of time. Because a round in boxing lasts for three minutes, boxers usually exercise for a similar period. A boxer may skip the rope for three minutes and then take a one-minute rest. Similarly, when a boxer spars he will do so for three minutes. This helps the body grow accustomed to exerting itself for a full three-minute round.

Although womens' boxing is a relatively new sport, female boxers must train every bit as hard as their male counterparts, to have any chance of success.

Boxing trainers, like George Francis shown here training with former world champion Frank Bruno, wear mitts to work on the boxer's combination punching.

Overtraining

Other types of training that boxers undergo include skill enhancement (which comprises shadow boxing, heavy and speed bag work), punch mitt work with the trainer and defensive drills. Conditioning is another important aspect of boxing training – this is when the boxer's work on the road comes into its own.

A typical training day for a boxer will see him run for the whole morning followed by a rest and then two or more hours in the gym. There is a fine line between training hard and overtraining – if a boxer overtrains he will not be able to function properly in the ring.

Diet

A good diet is of the utmost importance to a boxer. During the 1950s the USA's heavyweight contender 'Two Ton' Tony Galento used to boast that he prepared for his fights by drinking beer. Modern boxers are usually rather more fussy about what they eat and drink! Nowadays fighters eat five or six small meals a day. These consist of protein, often boiled chicken or fish, and carbohydrates, usually in the form of pasta.

Weight fact

Fighters may take drastic measures to lose weight prior to a fight. These include wearing rubber suits to 'sweat' off the pounds, chewing gum to produce saliva, eating only egg whites and running several times a day.

The support team

The modern boxer has a large team of people working with him to provide support and help in and out of the ring. The trainer has the closest relationship with the boxer. Often a former fighter himself, the trainer works with the boxer in the gym refining his skills and developing strategies for his next fight. Almost as important is the boxer's manager, who will organize his career path and try to ensure that the boxer is paid as much money as possible for his fights.

Seconds out

Once inside the ring, the importance of the boxer's team of **'seconds'** comes into play. A maximum of four seconds are permitted – these include the trainer and a **cuts man**, who wait at the corner of the ring and quickly provide a stool for their man to sit on at the end of each round. A good cuts man is essential – when a cut develops on a boxer's face the flow of blood must be stopped as quickly as possible or the boxer risks losing the fight. To do this, the cuts man applies pressure to the wound and uses adrenalin solution as a clotting agent. Another tool regularly used is the Enswell – this is a small piece of metal that helps to reduce swelling when the cuts man presses it against any lumps or bruises.

In the heat of battle the boxer's seconds can win or lose a fight. Each second has a specific job to do and teamwork is essential.

Emanuel Steward

In his youth, legendary boxing trainer Emanuel Steward (shown below, to the left of Lennox Lewis) sold ice cream to earn money. After an impressive **amateur** boxing career he chose not to turn professional and almost drifted out of boxing. In 1972, however, Steward started up his own boxing club at the Kronk Gym in Detroit. Over the next few decades Steward would become trainer to a record-breaking 29 world champions, including superstars such as Lennox Lewis and Oscar De La Hoya. Steward's biggest thrill, however, was when he won the National Golden Gloves amateur title in 1963: 'Nothing in my life has ever happened to exceed that moment,' he says.

A boxer's manager is one of the most important members of his team. Here Australian world champion Jeff Fenech (right) attends a press conference accompanied by his manager Don King.

Second fact

The Chief Second is the man who is in charge of the boxer's corner. This is usually the trainer, who coordinates the other seconds. During the rounds, seconds are not officially allowed to advise their fighters – although most do.

Attack!

In boxing there are four main types of punch: the **jab**, the straight punch, the **uppercut** and the **hook**. To punch correctly the boxer swivels his body along a central axis so that his full body weight is brought into the blow. This allows the boxer to punch harder and prevents 'arm punches' – weak shots that will quickly exhaust the boxer.

The jab

As well as scoring points, the jab should be used to keep the opponent off balance and on the defensive so that more powerful punches can be thrown. The jab is delivered with a slight clockwise movement of the fist, giving the punch greater snap. Boxers are taught to aim jabs at the chin of the opponent.

Power punches

The most basic power punch is the straight punch used by fighters such as the USA's Thomas Hearns. This is usually thrown behind the jab with the boxer pivoting his hips, allowing the other side of the body to act as a hinge. Hooks provide an element of surprise and are a favourite punch of fighters such as Mike Tyson and Roy Jones Jr. These punches are aimed towards the side of the opponent's chin, with the arm in the shape of a hook and the weight of the boxer resting on his back foot.

The uppercut can also be a very effective punch. This is achieved when the boxer shifts his weight to his right hip and punches in an upward motion. The uppercut is particularly effective against shorter opponents and was used to devastating effect by fighters such as US world heavyweight champion Joe Frazier.

British world champion Joe Calzaghe's left jab is one of the super-middleweight division fighter's most feared weapons.

Footwork

To be able to punch correctly, a boxer must work constantly in the gym on his **footwork**. In boxing, the feet act as an anchor for punches. Having the feet in the correct position allows the boxer to punch with power. In the most basic stance in boxing, the fighter rests his body weight on the front foot. The back leg is bent slightly, allowing the boxer to adjust his posture according to whether he is defending or attacking. A boxer is taught to move forward by sliding his feet along the ground, so that his stance does not change and he is always ready to throw or defend punches.

Julio Cesar Chavez

A pressure fighter is a boxer who constantly throws attacking punches until his opponent eventually wilts under the onslaught. Mexico's Julio Cesar Chavez (shown here on the right with Oscar De la Hoya) was one of the most successful pressure fighters of all time. In a career that spanned twenty-one years, Chavez won his first 90 bouts and was world champion in four different weight divisions during the 1980s. Chavez was a powerhouse of energy and would throw hundreds of punches every round.

Defence

A successful boxer must have a good defence. Although the easiest way of avoiding a punch is simply to step out of range, the good boxer learns to adjust his body so that he can throw **counter-punches**. Catching a punch in the palm of the hand or deflecting a punch with a short cuffing movement best defends the **jab**. Straight punches are defended in several ways: in the shoulder block the boxer shifts his weight on to the back foot and turns his body right to catch the punch high on the shoulder. Rolling with the punches is a more aggressive form of defence; here the boxer pivots to the right to slip his head under the punch so that he is able to counter-punch.

Bobbing and weaving

One of the best ways of avoiding an opponent's punches is to 'bob and **weave**'. Here the boxer tucks his head behind his gloves and uses his waist as a pivot. In this way the boxer is able to keep his head constantly moving while also protecting his body with his elbows. The boxer can then march forward and throw punches of his own.

One of the finest exponents of bobbing and weaving was the USA's Floyd Patterson, heavyweight champion from 1956–61. Patterson became the youngest-ever heavyweight champion when, aged 21 years and 10 months, he knocked out Archie Moore in Chicago, on 30 November, 1956.

The USA's Floyd Patterson was a master of bobbing and weaving. His characteristic stance earned him the nickname 'The Rabbit'.

Covering up

The best way to defend from **uppercuts** or **hooks** is to tuck in the elbows to protect the body. When a punch is thrown the boxer is then able to use the forearm to block. When a boxer is under prolonged pressure the best defence is to 'cover up'. There are three basic ways of doing this: in the Half Cover the boxer shifts his weight to his right foot and hides his chin behind the left shoulder, holding his right hand high; in the Double Arm Cover the boxer holds both gloves to his face and protects his body with his elbows; in the Cross Arm Guard the boxer crosses his arms and uses the right to protect the chin and the left to protect his body.

The best way for a boxer to protect himself from punches is to use his arms, fists and elbows as a shield.

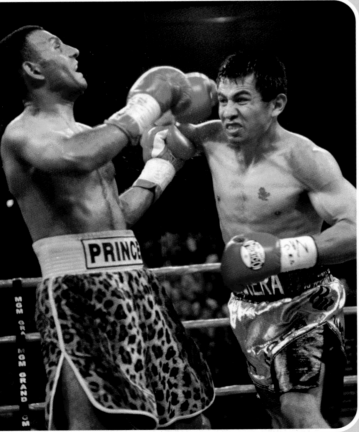

Defensive king

Mexico's Marco Antonio Barrera (shown here on the right) is rated one of the finest fighters in the world in any weight division. Born in 1974, Barrera combines devastating power with a solid defence that is almost impossible to penetrate. World champion at featherweight, Barrera's most impressive victory was an emphatic points decision over the previously unbeaten 'Prince' Naseem Hamed of the UK (left).

Developing a knockout punch

Two boxers can be the same height, the same build and the same weight but one is often able to punch harder than the other. An old saying in boxing states: 'You cannot teach power. Either a fighter is born with it or not.' But this is only partially true. While some fighters do seem to possess a natural knockout punch, there are a number of different things that a boxer can do to improve his punching power. Useful exercises for this include bench presses and squat thrusts which strengthen the abdominal muscles, the source of a boxer's punching power.

Anchoring the feet

One of the things that often prevents boxers from hitting powerfully is their stance. Some boxers like to stay on their toes and remain mobile so that they can avoid punches. This means that they find it difficult to gain the necessary leverage to throw big punches. A heavy hitter, however, has a different style. He will plant his feet firmly on the ground so that he can use the floor as leverage to get more of his body weight behind the punch. Big punchers are committed to the punch. This means that the boxer is not worried about trying to block any punches that may come his way. Instead, he is more interested in throwing his own big 'bombs'. He hopes that although he is sure to get hit during the course of the fight, he will hit harder than his opponent.

Fearsome fact

Panama's Roberto Duran boxed in the lightweight division in the 1970s and punched so hard that he once knocked out a horse. His brutal reputation terrified other fighters and won him world titles at four different weights: 'There's only one legend. That's me,' he said.

The USA's 'Big' George Foreman (right) is history's most powerful puncher. He won his second world title aged 45.

Knockout king

A boxer wishing to develop a knockout punch could follow the example of Puerto Rico's Felix 'Tito' Trinidad. He was one of the most ferocious punchers in the world and knocked out nine of his first ten opponents.

Trinidad's incredible power began in his feet, as he stood with them wide apart for maximum leverage. The power created by this leverage flowed up through his muscular legs into his upper body and finally into his fists, which were thrown by twisting his body at the hips. During the 1990s this raw punching power enabled Trinidad to capture world titles in the welterweight and light-middleweight divisions.

Retired Puerto Rican knockout king Felix Trinidad is a modern legend. Thirty-four of Tito's opponents ended the fight seeing stars.

All-time great Larry Holmes gives fellow American Ray Mercer a taste of his classic right hand.

Boxing's biggest hitters – the all-time greatest knockout ratio			
Name	Won-Lost-Drawn	Knockouts	%
George Foreman, USA, heavyweight (1969–97)	76-5-0	68	89%
Julian Jackson, USA, light-middleweight (1981–98)	55-6-0	49	89%
Mike Tyson, USA, heavyweight (1985–)	50-4-0	44	88%
Felix Trinidad, Puerto Rico, welterweight (1990–2002)	41-1-0	34	82%
Thomas Hearns, USA, light-middleweight (1977–2000)	59-5-1	46	78%
Archie Moore, USA, light-heavyweight (1935–63)	182-24-9	129	71%

Sparring

Sparring is one of the most important aspects of a boxer's preparation. In the build-up to a fight a boxer will undergo dozens, sometimes hundreds of rounds of sparring. Usually held in a full-size ring erected in the gym, sparring gives a boxer the opportunity to work on weaknesses in his technique or enables him to fine-tune his fight plan. The boxer's opponents in these sparring sessions are called sparring partners. Sometimes former champions themselves, but often up-and-coming fighters looking to gain experience, sparring partners are paid a fee to put the boxer through his paces.

Strengths and weaknesses

Sparring sessions are usually separated into three-minute rounds. Prior to the sessions, sparring partners are instructed by the boxer's

Sparring is probably the most important aspect of a fighter's training routine. Laila Ali, daughter of the legendary Muhammad Ali, is just as dedicated to sparring as her father was in his prime.

trainer to work on specific aspects of boxing. If, for example, a boxer has a weak defence, the sparring partner will be required to attack. Similarly, if a boxer wishes to hone his offensive skills, the sparring partner will be asked to concentrate on defence. Often, however, sparring allows boxers a valuable opportunity to simply fight. In doing so, the boxer ensures that his reflexes will not be dulled by inactivity before the fight.

In-fighting fact

In-fighting is an essential technique when a boxer is up against an opponent with greater reach. Moving in close allows the boxer to throw short **hooks** and **uppercuts** that eventually wear the opponent out.

Muhammad Ali

World heavyweight champion Muhammad Ali (above right) would often allow sparring partners to freely hit him during sparring sessions. Round after round would go by and Ali would simply lean back against the ropes, soaking up punishment. The boxer's tactics often bemused onlookers, who came away shocked by how poor Ali looked. History, however, proved that Ali knew exactly what he was doing. In his 1974 fight with George Foreman, Ali regained the world title by allowing Foreman to throw punch after punch at him as he lay on the ropes. By the eighth round Foreman was exhausted by his exertions and Ali was able to knock him out!

Safety

Boxing is a very dangerous sport and over the course of their career it is rare for a boxer not to suffer some form of injury. These range from bumps and abrasions, to broken hands and even brain damage. Taking continual punches to the head has a long-term effect: over time, a boxer's speech may become slurred and his reflexes dulled in a condition commonly known as 'punch drunk'. This physical and mental deterioration can continue into old age. Over the years, the safety aspect of boxing has been improved. Nowadays it is rare for a boxer to suffer serious injury in the ring, although tragedies sometimes cannot be prevented.

The dangers in boxing

These are the most common injuries that a boxer can suffer:

- head trauma and concussion – this can occur when a boxer is knocked out during a fight

- lacerations – these usually occur around the eyes and if a fighter has suffered a deep cut that needs stitches, it may re-open in later fights

- abdominal pain – caused by punches to the stomach

- bone and joint pain – brought on by the hundreds of punches that a boxer throws during a fight

- dislocated shoulders and detached retinas in the eye.

If a fighter shows signs of significant injury the referee will immediately stop the fight.

Miracle man

In 1991 British middleweight boxer Michael Watson (centre) suffered severe brain damage during his title fight with Chris Eubank. Watson lay in a coma for 40 days and was close to death. This prompted British boxing authorities to introduce a number of procedures that made boxing much safer in the UK. When Watson finally awoke, he had lost the use of his limbs and could not even speak. Watson's road to recovery was long and hard. Slowly he regained his movement and his speech returned. More than a decade later Watson was fit enough to complete the London Marathon – it took him six days of walking. It was a remarkable recovery.

Safety regulations

Fortunately for boxers, great strides have been made in relation to safety in boxing. Nowadays a doctor is always at hand during a fight. If a boxer is in distress the doctor will step in and stop the fight. To prevent brain damage occurring, oxygen is kept at the ringside. If a fighter is injured this will be quickly administered and the boxer will be rushed to an ambulance and then to hospital. Boxers also undergo regular medicals and brain scans. If any irregularities show up on the scans the boxer is no longer allowed to fight.

If boxers do not take regular brain scans they risk losing their boxing licence and the right to fight.

Injury fact

In 1973 Muhammad Ali suffered a broken jaw during a fight with fellow American Ken Norton. Suffering terrible pain, Ali managed to last the full twelve rounds with Norton, before losing a close points decision.

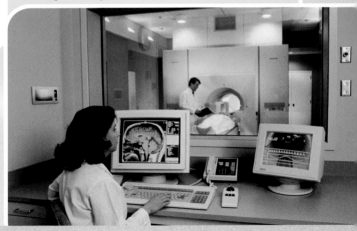

Devising a fight plan

During his career a boxer will meet many different types of opponents. Some will be heavier and stronger than he is; others will be taller or shorter. Some will be aggressive; others will be defensive **counter-punchers**. All of the boxer's opponents will have their own unique style that must be mastered. The boxer's support team will provide suggestions as to how to counter different types of opponent. The boxer's trainer works on particular aspects of the boxer's style, such as practising the **uppercut** for smaller opponents, and **jabbing** and keeping on the move against stronger opponents.

Counter measures

A boxer often studies videotapes of upcoming opponents. This enables him to highlight opponents' strengths and weaknesses. In general, however, the following tactics are regarded as the most effective:

- against a tall opponent it is best to keep moving while trying to dodge his punches; a smaller opponent is best countered by moving to the side and throwing uppercuts and **hooks**

- against a jabber it is best to put pressure on the opponent while moving the body from side to side

- a heavy puncher is countered by circling the ring and launching surprise attacks

- a counter-puncher can be nullified by forcing him to lead with the punches while feinting.

Using the uppercut is a good way of countering a smaller opponent.

The USA's Michael Moorer was the first southpaw (see page 35) to be crowned heavyweight champion.

Southpaw

No boxer likes to face a southpaw. A southpaw is a left-handed boxer who jabs with his right hand and punches with his left – the mirror opposite of a right-handed 'orthodox' fighter. Southpaws are difficult to fight because a boxer is taught to defend himself against right-handed opponents. When he fights a southpaw it is almost like learning to box again from scratch. Southpaws also have another advantage – they themselves have been taught to fight against right-handed boxers.

Southpaws are best handled by circling to the left and using the left hook to counter their jab. Some of boxing's greatest fighters have been southpaws. These include US middleweight champion Marvin Hagler and US heavyweight champion Michael Moorer.

The 'A Force'

Britain's Audley Harrison (right) is a southpaw who plans to follow in the footsteps of his illustrious predecessors George Foreman, Joe Frazier, Lennox Lewis and Muhammad Ali. All of these men won an Olympic gold medal and then went on to be world heavyweight champions. Born in London in 1971, Harrison completed the first part of this dream by winning the heavyweight gold medal at the 2000 Sydney Olympics. Standing two metres tall, the 'A Force' is a tricky left-hander who can box as well as punch. In the three years since he turned professional in 2001, he won all of his fights on the way to achieving his ambition. 'I get inspired every day by different people and it drives me on,' says Harrison.

Scoring points

Professional championship boxing matches are decided by the **10-point Must System**. First set up by the WBC in 1968, the system allows each boxer to score a maximum of ten points per round, with credit being given to a boxer who scores a knockdown. In this system a boxer winning a close round receives a score of ten points and his opponent nine. If he scores a knockdown he is again awarded ten points but his opponent receives only eight. Two knockdowns further reduce the points awarded to his opponent; after three knockdowns in a round the fight is automatically stopped. Boxers are given ten points apiece if the round is drawn.

Looking good fact

Boxers learn quickly how to influence the judges. Some will purposefully launch an impressive attack right at the end of a round so that this aggression will be fresh in the judges' minds. This is known as 'looking good' for the judges.

The target area

A boxer scores points by hitting the 'target' area with the knuckle part of his gloved fist. The target area comprises the front and sides of the head, and the chest area. The boxer is not allowed to hit the back of the head or body, or below the belt. If he does so he will receive a **warning** from the **referee** followed by point deductions for repeated infringements. Extra points are also awarded for defensive skill, clean punching and movement in the ring. Generally, however, boxing judges will reward aggressive fighters – in a close fight the boxer who has been the most aggressive will often be declared the victor.

The man in the middle

Referees are often referred to as the 'fourth official'. This is because there are also three boxing judges in

This diagram shows the target area of the body. A boxer scores points by throwing punches at this area.

Ring officials

Besides the referee, there are a bewildering number of officials at the ringside, each with a particular job to do:

- The supervisor briefs the referee and judges, and is responsible for declaring the result of the fight.

- Two inspectors are present at the ringside to check that no rules are broken.

- The timekeeper is responsible for ensuring that rounds last exactly three minutes. He also counts to ten when a fighter is knocked **down**.

- The official doctor can stop the fight if one of the boxers is injured.

- Three judges add up the points for each round.

championship boxing who watch the fight from ringside and keep their own points tally. At the end of each round their scorecards are handed in to the ring supervisor, who adds up the point totals. Judges are often former referees themselves and are appointed by boxing's governing bodies after passing a stringent examination. The judges' decisions can sometimes be controversial. In 1999 a government investigation was held in the USA to probe the draw between heavyweight champion Evander Holyfield and Lennox Lewis – most observers believed that Lewis had clearly won the fight.

Ala Villamor of the Philippines is counted out by referee Mills Lane.

The day of the fight

'I am so totally prepared for the fight that I just can't wait to get into the ring,' revealed American IBF heavyweight champion Chris Byrd the day before winning against Evander Holyfield in 2002. Boxers prepare for their fights in a variety of ways. Some, such as Byrd, prefer a quiet approach: a short run in the morning and a light meal at lunchtime. Others, such as the American former WBC heavyweight champion Oliver McCall get ready in more unusual ways. McCall warms up for his fights by bursting into tears! Some claim that this helps him to relieve the tension of the pre-fight build-up.

Winding down

A few days before a fight, boxers begin to slow down their training routine. Instead of a heavy sparring session, the boxer simply goes for a run and undergoes light training for three rounds. He will then take a short nap, allowing his body to rest before the coming exertions. Each boxer has his own individual routine on the day of the fight but most arrive at the fight venue with about an hour to spare. They are then given a massage to loosen the tension and take some final advice from their trainer.

Many boxers, such as the UK's featherweight champion Naseem Hamed, like to unwind by playing loud dance music. As the fight approaches the boxer makes final preparations and his hands are carefully wrapped in bandages. Finally, a doctor checks the boxer and his team are given instructions by the **referee** before being led into the arena.

On the morning of a fight, middleweight British boxer Nigel Benn would often spend hours at the hairdressers!

The sleepy champion

With less than an hour to go before the biggest fight of his career, heavyweight champion Lennox Lewis promptly fell asleep in his dressing room. This happened in 1999 during Lewis's build up to his historic rematch with Evander Holyfield. Now retired, the reflective Lewis is also a keen chess player who played up to four hours a day when in training. 'It's like boxing: there's a strategy,' he says. 'You have to decide what move to use, or what combination of moves.'

Former British chess champion Nigel Short is a fan of Lewis. 'He clearly has the right ideas, and plays a lot of very logical moves,' reveals Short. 'But if he offers you a draw in a menacing tone of voice, accept.'

America's Tommy Morrison undergoes a training session in the gym before a fight.

The pain barrier

Your muscles are on fire and you fight for every breath. Your limbs feel like lead and you are ready to collapse from exhaustion. This is what every fighter must overcome in order to earn the right to be called a great champion – the pain barrier. The pain barrier is a term used to describe the sensation of asphyxia – or oxygen deprivation – that occurs during violent physical exertion. When an athlete hits the pain barrier his muscles tighten and become very painful when he tries to move them.

Acid test

Pain is one of the things that separate boxing from many other sports. Pain is something that a boxer conditions himself to live with through rigorous exercise that takes his body to the limits. During physical activity the body produces a chemical known as lactic acid; under the microscope this appears as tiny salt-like particles that lodge into the muscle fibres. Sessions with the heavy bag are a particularly useful method of lengthening the lactic acid threshold. Many boxers combine such drills with training trips to high-altitude locations, where the air is thinner and physical training requires greater effort.

Both male and female boxers have to be able to fight through the pain barrier. Here Jane Couch tackles Sharon Anyos during a WBF boxing round in London.

Hitting the zone

During a fight, a boxer will sometimes experience what is known as a 'second wind'. At the point of physical collapse he will suddenly feel full of renewed energy: his arms and legs will move freely and he will be able to box as well as he did during the first round. The second wind occurs when the body produces chemicals called endorphins. As well as giving the boxer extra energy, endorphins also help to dull pain and give the boxer a feeling of euphoria. In America this is known as 'hitting the zone'.

Pickled fists fact

Another of the most common problems in boxing is hand pain. In the past, boxers such as Australia's featherweight champion Jeff Fenech soaked their hands in vinegar in an attempt to prevent it!

Third world war

On the night of 18 May 2002 America's Mickey Ward (right) and Arturo Gatti (left) were involved in one of the most punishing fights of modern times. Boxing critics dubbed the encounter the 'fight of the century'. During the epic battle both men were pushed past the pain barrier. In the ninth round Gatti was knocked to the floor by Ward, who threw literally hundreds of punches at his opponent. Just six months later the pair fought another hard fight with Gatti earning the points verdict this time. Finally, a tremendous third fight in 2003 saw Gatti triumph once more. Ward immediately announced his retirement from the ring. 'I just couldn't believe how strong this guy was,' said Gatti. 'He was hitting me with those body shots and I can take a shot to the body, but they were making my legs even more tired.'

Being a champion

For more than a decade, the USA's Roy Jones Jr has been rated as one of the best fighters in the world. Unusually, he has claimed world titles in four separate weight divisions and in 2003 won a heavyweight title with an emphatic points victory over fellow American John Ruiz. In doing so, Jones became the first middleweight champion to claim a heavyweight title since Britain's Bob Fitzsimmons way back in 1897. Jones, who combines devastating punching power with exceptional ring craft, is a truly great fighter.

Multiple champion

Jones began his professional career in 1989 after a distinguished **amateur** career that included a silver medal at the 1988 Seoul Olympic Games. Boxing as a middleweight, Jones steadily climbed the rankings before winning the IBF title in 1993. Within a year Jones had also claimed the IBF super-middleweight title, which he defended five times before moving up in weight for a second time. In 1996 Jones won the WBC light-heavyweight crown but lost it in his first defence match after being disqualified for hitting opponent Montell Griffin when he was **down**.

In 2003 Roy Jones Jr capped his career by becoming WBA heavyweight champion.

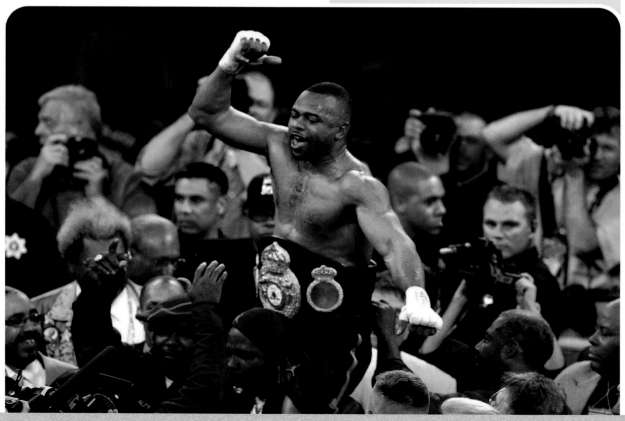

This disappointment proved to be only a minor blip on Jones's career path. In his next fight, Jones regained the WBC light-heavyweight crown from Griffin and began a run of defences that culminated with him unifying the title in 2001. Amazingly, Jones became the only fighter ever to hold WBC, WBA, IBF, IBO and WBF versions of the same title. Not content with being a contender for greatest light-heavyweight of all time, Jones next turned his attention to the heavyweight division. The defeat of Ruiz earned Jones the WBA heavyweight title and a place in the history books.

The quiet champion

Unlike controversial boxers such as Mike Tyson, Roy Jones Jr takes great pains to ensure that he is a positive role model for his legions of fans. The softly spoken Jones has brought a dignity to boxing that has not been seen since the days of American heavyweight champion Joe Louis in the 1940s. Jones, who has also played professional basketball for a number of teams in the USA, began boxing at the age of ten. 'The one thing from boxing that I learned was how it felt to win,' he says. 'That was the best thing in life for me, to be able to come home and say – I won.'

Roy Jones's career highlights

Roy Jones Jr (right) is a positive role model to thousands of youngsters.

1988 Wins Olympic middleweight silver medal.

1993 Wins IBF middleweight title.

1994 Wins IBF super-middleweight title.

1996 Wins vacant WBC light-heavyweight title.

1997 Loses and regains WBC light-heavyweight title.

2001 Unifies the light-heavyweight title.

2003 Wins the WBA heavyweight title.

Boxing greats

Here are some facts and figures about great fighters and fights. This includes some of the less well-known achievements of boxers through the ages.

Most world titles
5 – 'Sugar' Ray Leonard
5 – Thomas Hearns

Most world title fights
27 – Joe Louis

Most world title fight wins
26 – Joe Louis

Oldest world champion
45 – George Foreman

Youngest world champion
17 – Wilfred Benitez

Longest reigning champion
11 years 252 days – Joe Louis

Shortest reigning champion
33 days – Tony Canzoneri

Heaviest world champion
270lb – Primo Carnera

Tallest world champion
Ernie Terrell – 2 metres

Shortest world title fight
45 seconds – Al McCoy v George Chip, middleweight, 1914

45 seconds – Lloyd Honeyghan v Gene Hatcher, welterweight, 1987

Most knockdowns in world title fights
14 – Vic Toweel v Danny O'Sullivan, bantamweight, 1950

Largest purse
$34 million, paid to Lennox Lewis for his fight against Mike Tyson in 2002.

Olympic Champions

Super Heavyweight		
Date	Name	Nationality
1984	Tyrell Biggs	USA
1988	Lennox Lewis	Canada
1992	Roberto Balado	Cuba
1996	Wladimir Klitschko	Ukraine
2000	Audley Harrison	UK
2004	Alexander Povetkin	Russia

Heavyweight		
Date	Name	Nationality
1984	Henry Tillman	USA
1988	Ray Mercer	USA
1992	Felix Savon	Cuba
1996	Felix Savon	Cuba
2000	Felix Savon	Cuba
2004	Odlanier Solis Fonte	Cuba

Light Heavyweight		
Date	Name	Nationality
1984	Anton Josipovic	Yugoslavia
1988	Andrew Maynard	USA
1992	Torsten May	Germany
1996	Vassili Jirov	Kazakhstan
2000	Alexander Lebziak	Russia
2004	Andre Ward	USA

Middleweight		
Date	Name	Nationality
1984	Joon-Sup Shin	South Korea
1988	Henry Maske	East Germany
1992	Ariel Hernandez	Cuba
1996	Ariel Hernandez	Cuba
2000	Jorge Gutierrez	Cuba
2004	G. Gaydarbekov	Russia

Light Middleweight

Date	Name	Nationality
1984	Frank Tate	USA
1988	Si-Hun Park	South Korea
1992	Juan Lemus	Cuba
1996	David Reid	USA
2000	Yermakhan Ibraimov	Kazakhstan
2004	G. Gaydarbekov	Russia

Welterweight

Date	Name	Nationality
1984	Mark Breland	USA
1988	Robert Wangila	Kenya
1992	Michael Carruth	Ireland
1996	Oleg Saitov	Russia
2000	Oleg Saitov	Russia
2004	Bakhtiyar Artayev	Kazakhstan

Light Welterweight

Date	Name	Nationality
1984	Jerry Page	USA
1988	Viatcheslav Janovski	Soviet Union
1992	Hector Vinent	Cuba
1996	Hector Vinent	Cuba
2000	Mayhamadkadyz Abdullaev	Uzbekistan
2004	M. Boonjumnong	Thailand

Lightweight

Date	Name	Nationality
1984	Pernell Whitaker	USA
1988	Andreas Zuelow	East Germany
1992	Oscar De La Hoya	USA
1996	Hocine Soltani	Algeria
2000	Mario Kindelan	Cuba
2004	Mario Kindelan	Cuba

Featherweight

Date	Name	Nationality
1984	Meldrick Taylor	USA
1988	Giovanni Parisi	Italy
1992	Andreas Tews	Germany
1996	Somluck Kamsing	Thailand
2000	Bekzat Sattarkhanov	Kazakhstan
2004	Alexei Tichtchenko	Russia

Bantamweight

Date	Name	Nationality
1984	Maurizo Stecca	Italy
1988	Kennedy McKinney	USA
1992	Joel Casamayor	Cuba
1996	Istvan Kovacs	Hungary
2000	Guillermo Ridondeaux	Cuba
2004	G. Rigondeaux	Cuba

Flyweight

Date	Name	Nationality
1984	Steven McCrory	USA
1988	Kwang-Sun Kim	South Korea
1992	Su Choi-Choi	North Korea
1996	Maikro Romero	Cuba
2000	Wijan Ponlid	Thailand
2004	Yuriorkis Toledano	Cuba

Light Flyweight

Date	Name	Nationality
1972	Gyorgy Gedo	Hungary
1976	Jorge Hernandez	Cuba
1980	Shamil Sabyrov	Soviet Union
1984	Paul Gonzalez	USA
1988	Ivalio Hristov	Bulgaria
1992	Rogelio Marcelo	Cuba
1996	Daniel Petrov	Bulgaria
2000	Brahim Asloum	France
2004	Yan B. Varela	Cuba

Nationality fact

Although Lennox Lewis was born in the UK, he moved to Canada as a youngster and fought as an amateur for that country. After winning the Olympic gold medal for Canada in 1988, Lewis returned to the country of his birth to begin his professional career fighting for the UK.

Glossary

amateur
a boxer who is not paid a purse, or prize money, to fight

chief second
the person who provides advice and assistance during a bout, usually the trainer

combination
punches thrown in sequence, such as a left jab, followed by a straight right, followed by a left hook

counter-punch
a counterattack begun immediately after an opponent throws a punch

cup
the equipment protecting a boxer's genitals, lower abdomen and lower back

cuts man
corner man whose job it is to stop the bleeding of cuts or reduce swelling to the face

down
a boxer is considered down if he touches the floor with anything other than his feet or if they go outside the ropes from a blow

eight-count
when a boxer is hurt or floored, the referee counts to eight. If the referee decides that the boxer is unable to continue fighting after this count, the contest is adjudged to be over.

footwork
the way a boxer moves and plants his feet to enable him to be in position for throwing punches and defending

foul
an infringement of boxing rules

gum shield or **mouthpiece**
a piece of plastic used to protect a fighter's teeth and prevent him from biting his tongue

hook
a short power punch in which the boxer swings from the shoulder with his elbow bent, bringing his fist from the side toward the centre

in-fighting
boxing at close range

jab
a quick straight punch thrown with the lead hand

promoter
the person or organization that organizes, advertises, produces and conducts a professional boxing match

Queensbury Rules
the rules by which boxing is governed, established by the marquis of Queensbury in 1867

referee
the official who ensures the bout is clean and fair, and who makes sure the boxers are physically able to box after taking a punch

second
a person aside from the coach who gives a boxer assistance or advice between rounds

standing eight second count
when a fighter is in distress the referee stops the fight and counts to eight so that he may decide if the boxer is able to continue

10-point Must System
the scoring system used in boxing. To win the round a boxer must score 10 points.

three-knockdown rule
a rule that states that a boxer is disqualified if he is knocked down 3 times in a single round

uppercut
a powerful upward punch that comes up beneath an opponent's guard

warning
given by the referee to a boxer who commits a serious foul, or receives three cautions. Three warnings in a bout means disqualification.

weave
turn and twist to avoid punches

Resources

Further reading

Boxer's Start-up: Beginner's Guide to Boxing (Start-up Sports), Doug Werner (Tracks Publishing, 1988)
Everything you need to know to begin boxing.

The Illustrated Encyclopaedia Of World Boxing, Peter Arnold (WH Smith Books, 1989)
The complete reference book of boxing and boxers.

Top 10 Heavyweight Boxers, Ron Knapp (Enslow Publishers, 1997)
Profiles the lives and careers of ten of the greats. Includes Muhammad Ali, George Foreman, Joe Louis and Mike Tyson.

Useful websites

Boxing Canada
www.boxing.ca

USA Boxing
www.usaboxing.org

World Boxing Association
www.wbaonline.com

I.B.F.
www.ibf-usba-boxing.com

Women's I.B.F.
www.wibf.org

Organizations

UK
Amateur Boxing Association of England Ltd
Crystal Palace National Sports Centre
London
SE19 2BB
UK

USA
USA Amateur Boxing Inc
1 Olympic Plaza
Colorado Springs
CO 80909 5776
USA

Australia
Amateur Boxing Association of Australia
State Association House
1 Stuart Street
Adelaide
SA 5000
Australia

New Zealand
NZ Boxing Association
PO Box 24148
Manners Street
Wellington
New Zealand

Disclaimer

All the Internet addresses (URLs) given in this book were valid as at 1 may 2004. However, due to the dynamic nature of the Internet, some addresses may have changed, or sites may have changed or ceased to exist since publication. While the author and Publishers regret any inconvenience this may cause readers, no responsibility for any such changes can be accepted by either the author or the Publishers.

Index

Ali, Muhammad 11, 12, 16, 31, 33, 35
alphabet men 10
amateur boxing 14, 16, 42
Armstrong, Henry 13

bare-knuckle boxing 7
Barrera, Marco Antonio 27
brain damage 33

Chavez, Julio Cesar 9, 25
concussion 32
conditioning 21
cuts 22, 32
cuts man 22

defence 26–27
diet 21

equipment 18–19
exercises 14–15, 18, 28

footwork 25
Foreman, George 28, 29, 31, 35

Gatti, Arturo 41
gloves 6, 16
gum shields 19

fitness 14, 15

hand wrapping 19, 38
Harrison, Audley 35
head guards 16, 17
history of boxing 6–11

injuries 32–33
interval training 20

Jones Jr, Roy 42–43
judges 17, 36, 37

King, Don 11, 23
knockout punches 28, 29
Kronk Gym 15, 23

Lewis, Lennox 4, 5, 11, 16, 23, 35, 37, 39

managers 22, 23

Olympic Games 6, 16, 35, 42, 44–45

pain barrier 40
promoters 11
protective vests 16, 17, 19
punch bags 18
punching 24–25

Queensbury Rules 8

referee 8, 9, 36, 37, 38
ring officials 37
rules 6, 8

scoring points 17, 36, 37
seconds 22, 23
southpaw 35
sparring 30–31, 38

stance 28
Steele, Richard 9
Stevenson, Teofilo 16
Steward, Emanuel 15, 23
Sullivan, John L. 7, 8
support team 22–23, 34

tactics 34
target area 36
10-point Must System 36
trainers 21, 22, 23
training 20–21, 38
Trinidad, Felix 29
Tyson, Mike 4, 5, 11, 24, 29, 43

Ward, Mickey 41
warming up 15, 38
Watson, Michael 33
weight divisions 4, 11, 12, 13, 29
women's boxing 11, 20, 40
World Boxing Association 10
world championships 10–11